Laziness:

How to Turn your Life Around with Proven Methods to Overcome Procrastination, Laziness, and Lack of Motivation

Anthony Heston

© Copyright 2018 by Anthony Heston

All rights reserved.

The follow eBook is reproduced below with the goal of providing information that is as accurate and reliable as possible. Regardless, purchasing this eBook can be seen as consent to the fact that both the publisher and the author of this book are in no way experts on the topics discussed within and that any recommendations or suggestions that are made herein are for entertainment purposes only. Professionals should be consulted as needed prior to undertaking any of the action endorsed herein.

This declaration is deemed fair and valid by both the American Bar Association and the Committee of Publishers Association and is legally binding throughout the United States.

Furthermore, the transmission, duplication or reproduction of any of the following work including specific information will be considered an illegal act irrespective of if it is done electronically or in print. This extends to creating a secondary or tertiary copy of the work or a recorded copy and is only allowed with express written consent from the Publisher. All additional right reserved.

The information in the following pages is broadly considered to be a truthful and accurate account of facts and as such any inattention, use or misuse of the information in question by the reader will render any resulting actions solely under their purview. There are no scenarios in which the publisher or the original author of this work can be in any fashion deemed liable for any hardship or damages that may befall them after undertaking information described herein.

Additionally, the information in the following pages is intended only for informational purposes and should thus be thought of as universal. As befitting its nature, it is presented without assurance regarding its prolonged validity or interim quality. Trademarks that are mentioned are done without written consent and can in no way be considered an endorsement from the trademark holder.

Table of Contents

Introduction 7

Chapter 1: Fighting is Not the Answer 15

Chapter 2: The Unconscious Mind 19

Chapter 3: The Word Lazy is Lazy 31

Chapter 4: Cognitive Reframing 53

Chapter 5: Activity and Nutrition 67

Conclusion 87

Introduction

When it comes to finding the happiness you want out of life and achieving your long-term goals, the simple fact of the matter is that hard work will, eventually, be required. In most cases, the only thing that separates you from the most successful and powerful people in the world is the fact that they have learned to focus their untapped potential by overcoming their laziness.

Laziness - The quality of being unwilling to work or use energy; idleness

Procrastination - The action of delaying or postponing something

Often, they are thought of as the same things, but they are separate and in many cases not interchangeable. Procrastinators, put off what needs to be done. They procrastinate the chore or errand they need to attend. Laziness can mean not wanting to reach down to pick up some trash that fell from your pocket, or not wanting to wash the stack of dishes. They are really two different scenarios, but we often use the term lazy to describe both of them.

Although most of us possess a similar concept of what types of actions constitute laziness, it is still a subjective identifier. You may consider someone that only mows their lawn in two-week intervals lazy, while the old man down the street may think anything greater than four days between yard maintenance is lazy.

The truth is the word "lazy" is a lazy word because commonly, the term is used to dole out a snap judgment about another's habits or lifestyle. In this, we fail to acknowledge or identify the reasons why. Knowledge of circumstance, however, would lend an entirely different understanding. Therefore, circumstance holds the keys to surpassing that which is holding you back.

In this book, we will revitalize our understanding of laziness and procrastination. We will grow out of the habit of simply regarding someone as lazy or not lazy. We will recognize the prerequisites that enable procrastination and some methodology for reversing this inhibiting thought form. You will find that the information presented will be highly psychological and practical across multiple domains.

It's useful to see and examine these definitions so we can understand that the two terms are not critical, and though they are often used interchangeably, knowing them as being separate from one another will aid in your self-treatment.

In this book, we will be dissolving some of the negative energies and associations surrounding these terms. With this, we will be able to unlock a method of self-management with regards to postponing goals that are important. If you have already made up your mind about laziness and procrastination, I invite you to soften your attitudes and predispositions. My offering to you is a more constructive and cooperative relationship with lazy tendencies. You will soon discover that there are no lazy people, and procrastinators do not exist. Rather, these behaviors affect us all for different reasons and at different intervals. I doubt anyone would debate that laziness affects each of us at a certain point, but most of my readers are interested in gaining more information and perspective concerning the interval that this occurs. If it is self-improvement you seek, it will be crucial that you allow yourself to be gentle, honest, fair, and introspective.

Before we dig in, I will begin by offering this foundational, yet simple, idea about the relationship between laziness and procrastination. An unwillingness to expend energy is one of the many reasons we choose procrastination or to procrastinate. This puts laziness under the umbrella of procrastination alongside many other justified reasons. We will discuss more about why they're justified in the following chapter. If we know that procrastination is simply the action of postponement, being critical when hearing the word procrastination is undue. Your decision to postpone an event or project is case and context dependent. Procrastination is a broad term that does not detail a certain reason for the postponement. The word simply expresses the choice to postpone, and in some cases, it may be the most intuitive one.

Laziness is an unwillingness to use energy. While the very concept of idleness is demonized by western culture, laziness is not an affliction, but rather a sign, a message, a symptom. Grounded individuals will:

- Observe symbols like this in their lives
- Accept that it is impacting them

- Recognize that it could happen to anybody given the context they are in at the moment then
- Seek to impact balance on the matter

Is not necessary to destroy or conquer undesirable actions, habits, and patterns. These perceived problems will always reincarnate. A method for cooperating and harmonizing with the conditions that cause laziness, and in turn procrastination, will surely change your life. You will see that laziness is a multifaceted issue with many contributing factors. Don't be discouraged. We will be refining some misconceptions. We will see that these misconceptions have blinded us to some simple truths that have been hidden in plain sight.

You will notice that these first few chapters will contain definitions and often make technical and subtle distinctions. It's important that we are careful of how we represent these concepts in our minds. These representations are our attitudes, and they will impact our behaviors. Consider having a job in which you do not enjoy the duties that fall outside of your skillset as opposed to work that you enjoyed and was surmountable by you. Negative associations with our topic will similarly leave you feeling discouraged and unable to enact change in your scenario and environment.

Regarding laziness as a weakness classified by a state of being perpetually unmotivated is a critical perspective and will be a disservice to you in your pursuance of task completion. We will discard this perception in favor of one that is more constructive.

Chapter 1:
Fighting is Not the Answer

Now that we know what laziness and procrastination are, we should also understand that they are not issues worth fighting against themselves. Laziness and procrastination are merely the tip of the iceberg. Even if we could fight them directly, what would we end up with? Another truth about the unconscious mind is that it is very subject oriented. Making an adversary of laziness only gives it more power and influence over your decisions and behaviors. This is because when choosing to fight against it, the subject we represent in our unconscious mind is laziness.

It does not matter that the goal is to fight against laziness; the mind will orient itself to the subject alone. This is because the subconscious mind is a creative builder. It ignores negating words; as its job is to create, not destroy. You may have heard the saying "what you resist persists," and this is why that saying is true. The things that we resist, we are telling our minds "no this" and "no that." Unfortunately, that is construed by the unconscious mind to mean, "build me more of this" and "get to work creating that." This is not a bad thing. We simply need to learn how to operate in accordance with it.

When we encounter laziness, we should identify the reason why laziness is being expressed. We then should work to balance the cause. With laziness and procrastination and all other undesirable behavior patterns, we should seek balance over annihilation, and cooperation over competition. A key character value that will unlock the door to this balancing and cooperative effort is acceptance.

Acceptance is recognizing an issue or an undesirable condition and consequently being able to conclude, "this is okay." Acceptance is a sort of tolerance in that way. It helps reestablish authority over the things we wish to resolve. Acceptance holds the power to transmute adversities into advantages. Accept.

Chapter 2:
The Unconscious Mind

Before we continue, it is highly important to emphasize the role the unconscious mind plays in these types of behaviors. Procrastination is one of many manifestations of the unconscious mind. It is true that the unconscious mind is elusive. We cannot be acutely aware of how it does what it does, and as the name implies, it is a portion of ourselves that is distinguished from conscious cognition. That being said, the unconscious portion of mind is definitely the larger portion of our minds. We all have a relationship with our unconscious selves. That's right, in this book, we are going to be understanding and engaging our unconscious mind, not as some abstract metaphorical machine that operates outside of our control, rather we will see it as the rest of ourselves that we already know and love.

The things we do, think, and experience impresses upon our unconscious minds, and the things that we feed into it, it processes, these things we feed into ourselves, we process on a deep level, then our unconscious self consequently impresses on us, shaping our decisions and perceptions.

If we have a circle that represents the mind, we can imagine the circle as being portioned into a small piece and one other very large piece. As you've already guessed, this smaller portion of the circle represents our conscious mind. Why does our conscious awareness lie inside this smaller portion? Well, how big of a piece do we really need? Since our unconscious mind is still part of the same circle, we are not being left out or omitted from any information. All information is a part of us. This unconscious mind is yours. It is you. It controls unconscious anatomical and biological processes, which means, you do. Maybe right now you are tense. Perhaps your breath is shallow. You weren't consciously tensing your muscles, however at the same time, no one other than you is. Right now, you can choose to take awareness of your breath and relax the tension in your body. This ability pervades all biological processes. We can consciously take control, or influence change in ourselves on a physical level given we have a strong enough connection, or relationship, with our unconscious mind.

"Dr. Kamler met Hof for the first time at the Rubin Museum in New York, where Hof was set to break another Guinness World Record, this time for remaining nearly naked in ice poured up to his neck.

Hof came out of the museum, stripped to his swim trunks and climbed in a 5-foot tall plexiglass container filled with ice. Once he got in, they poured more ice into the container until it reached his chin.

All the while, Dr. Ken Kamler monitored Hof from outside the tank.

Normally, when a person is exposed to freezing temperatures for a prolonged period of time, the body goes into survival mode, as its liquids begin to freeze.

Frostbite sets in, and in order to save the major organs, the body sacrifices blood flow to the extremities, cutting circulation from the fingers, toes, ears and nose to keep the blood flowing to the organs necessary for survival.

If not treated immediately, the damage to these extremities is irreversible. The other danger is hypothermia, an abnormally low body temperature.

At about 90 degrees, body functions start shutting down, and once that starts, you could be dead within minutes.

But Hof stayed in his tomb of ice for one hour and 12 minutes. Then, the ice was poured out of the tank, and Hof emerged, his skin still pink.

"He's not moving, he's not generating heat, he's not dressed for it, and he's immersed in ice water. And water will transmit heat 30 times faster than air. It literally sucks the life right out of you. And yet, despite all those negative factors, Wim Hof was very calm, very comfortable the entire time that he was immersed in that water," Kamler said.

It was a new entry for the Guinness World Records, but really, no one else out there seems able to compete with him. He just keeps breaking his own records."

- Joseph Angier, 7 March 2008, ABC News, Iceman on Everest: 'It Was Easy'

It has been proven that we can consciously influence autonomous systems in our body, but let's get back to the mind and our behaviors. The unconscious mind is a powerful part of who we are. Despite what we've come to understand about it so far, it is simply a place that we deeply think about things that are less important to us in a given moment. Ideally, we want to relate to this other side of ourselves so that we can pass information back-and-forth between the portions with the ease. A poor relationship with our unconscious will cause this exchange of information and emotion to flow without ease. This concept is directly related to the term disease. The mind and the body begin to fail in this scenario. There's plenty to say about this matter, but to keep it simple, I'll provide a metaphor that may be useful an understanding what goes on when there is a lack of synchronization between the two.

Imagine two people 'cutting it close' for time on the way to some appointment. They enter their vehicle at the same time, which terrifyingly is outfitted with two steering wheels on both driver and passenger sides, along with two sets of gas and brake pedals. They may both control the car, but there is a glass barrier between them and shields all verbal communication, and not that they mind, neither is paying attention to the others desires and agendas. Imagine how far this vehicle would be able to travel with both drivers having equal control and trying to steer it in different directions. Would you be a passenger? Hopefully, this somewhat illustrates the importance of coordinating the efforts of the mind.

When you look into a room, you may only notice your pet curled up and sleeping peacefully, but in reality, you perceive and an unconscionable amount of information and detail about the room. Your unconscious mind is almost like "Rain Man" counting the precise number of fibers in the carpet, or specks of dirt on the floor. Your mind is entirely conscious of everything present in the scene. The truth is, we don't need to know a comprehensive set of details about everything we encounter consciously. It is delegated to the unconscious mind for a useful purpose. Sometimes information is delegated due to relevance, other times information is sent to the unconscious for higher order thought processing.

Now that you understand the unconscious mind to be the other part of you that does the heavy lifting, you will be prepared later when we talk about never resisting, rumination, and other behavioral aspects of laziness and procrastination.

As soon as you commit to beginning your work, distractions will flood in from all corners of the earth. Like clockwork, people and circumstances will enter in to the equation in an effort to seemingly undermine your commitment to your task. The same distractions are never present when you actually have the free time to address them. In keeping with the theme of how to handle such adversities, we will not allow ourselves to get irritated or frustrated with this influx of new distractions. Instead, we will just recognize these new distractions and temptations as a signal or sign.

The convergence of external distractions at the precise moment you decide to begin work on your task may seem like some cruel trick the universe is trying to play on you or some test of your willpower. The truth is the emergence of these distractions does indeed come from your inner universe. They did not pop up out of nowhere just to distract you from your goal, rather, the way you identify new tasks changed as soon as you committed to a project requiring your special and undivided attention. That is, these distractions didn't come out of nowhere just to inhibit your progress. Your mind is choosing to classify these events that would have occurred regardless, as potential threats - distractions. Again, we will not look at this truth and frown. This operation of your unconscious mind is a powerful sign and indicator in which you can convert into inspiration and motivation toward your goal.

Say it is time to sit down and work on some homework that you been procrastinating, and it's due first thing tomorrow when you report to class. As soon as you sit down with your books and computer, the phone rings and you receive invitations to go out and have fun, this, along with five other imminent and urgent distractions. Instead of causing you stress, look on these distractions with a smile. Don't take the bait but recognize this truth: the quality and quantity of these distractions are directly correlated with the importance of completing the task you originally sat down to accomplish. This meaning, the weight of these distractions suggest the importance of completing your task.

Your unconscious mind has already calculated the expected gains made by completing this homework from the example. The anticipation of the success and self-gratification completing this task would bring, excites our unconscious mind. However, without understanding this operation of the mind, this excitement will be expressed in the form of seeking a postponement in covert ways. Our minds have the opportunity to be very cunning when we don't understand how they're performing.

The next time you commit to taking on a new task or goal only to be bombarded buy a plethora of tempting distractions, recognize that the weight of distractibility these tasks seem to have is invented by you. It's a communication from a deeper part of yourself that you're excited about the task at hand and that the completion of said task will have a positive and often profound impact on your present and future circumstances. Now, when the pesky distractions creep in, don't allow yourself to be frustrated, instead, you will say "I must be excited to complete such an important task. The weight of these distractions lies in proportion to how crucial it is that I accomplish my goal."

The motivation to complete your tasks has always been there, perhaps misidentified, but there nonetheless. Now that we understand what is going on better inside ourselves, we can harness this excitement because this excitement is energy generated from the anticipation of task completion. Doesn't this sound a lot like motivation?

Chapter 3:
The Word Lazy is Lazy

"There are always barriers. Recognizing those barriers— and viewing them as legitimate—is often the first step to breaking "lazy" behavior patterns.

It's really helpful to respond to a person's ineffective behavior with curiosity rather than judgment"

-E. Price, "Laziness Does Not Exist"

The simple fact of the matter is that it is easier for society to judge laziness rather than acknowledging the situational factors that most frequently tend to give rise to it. Give it a break. Use of the word lazy as a critical judgment doesn't do anyone any good. In fact, this use of the word lazy is, itself, lazy. The person passing judgment doesn't feel like using the energy to see and understand what the root cause is. It would only be then that they would be able to see this manifestation as something else entirely. There's always a cause for the things we do. Perhaps you are the one criticizing and guilting yourself. Cut yourself some slack, because to you, I say again: there is a good reason for why you are postponing or feeling unmotivated.

If a person's car breaks down, does that person then call their car lazy? While that would certainly be humorous, we typically do nothing of the sort as there is little to be gained by doing so. We know a car can break down for any number of reasons. It's a problem that will affect all cars at some point along the journey, and when the problem arises, we promptly identify and fix it. Proper knowledge of when and how to maintain the vehicle usually contributes to fewer breakdowns, however, not always. The car is a great metaphor for laziness and how it's misunderstood in popular culture. Not feeling the motivation to act on your goals doesn't mean that you are a lazy person. There is simply a problem to be identified and then fixed. Just like the car, you will be back on the road in no time. If you drive your car often, as many of us do, you understand why it's important to be acclimated with how to care for your car and provide preventative maintenance in order to keep it on the road. This same principle applies to you.

So many people are disgusted by excuses. It's hard to understand how the term got warped and twisted to have a negative connotation. An excuse is simply a reason for behaving in a certain way. Some say "save the excuses," or "I don't want to hear your excuses." These people do not want to know the reason(s) that themselves or others behave a certain way? Unconscionable. When we are able to understand the factors that contribute to our problem, we are able to treat and address them in others and ourselves. For this reason, dismissing someone else as being lazy is hypocritical. It's not that this type of person is incapable of understanding; they just choose not to expend any effort to understand. This expression represents their own relationship with the matter.

"I can't relate to lazy people. We don't speak the same language. I don't understand you. I don't want to understand you." –Kobe Bryant

"I'm chasing perfection." –Kobe Bryant

When we examine these statements spoken by Kobe Bryant using the information we have learned so far in this book, we can easily see what Kobe Bryant's mind has to share about the subject of laziness. Filled with contradiction, this statement is a prime example of the person that points the finger, yet hypocritically is a victim of his own judgments. "I don't want to understand you" directly suggests an unwillingness to use energy to understand himself and those around him. We know that the unconscious mind represents the larger portion of our thoughts and attitudes, and we also know that it does not process nor understand negating words. What, then, are the resulting ideas when we remove the negative words from this first quote?

I relate to lazy people. We speak the same language. I do understand you. I want to understand you.

"I'm chasing perfection." In this quote, Kobe at least admits that he is working toward perfection, suggesting he does indeed struggle with laziness and procrastination at times. Most importantly about this quote, however, is the attitude held by Kobe and many others. The idealization of perfection may seem virtuous at first, but in practice, it can cause low self-esteem and make one highly susceptible to procrastination. We will discuss this later in a section titled "Perfectionism."

Mental Dispositions

We understand that procrastination affects all of us at certain times over certain types of tasks and is nothing to be harsh or self-critical about. People procrastinate for a variety of reasons. Understandably, this calls for the deployment of multiple solutions. One way we will evaluate which solution to use will be to identify the characteristics of our personality and mental state. Certain personality types don't face as much of a struggle with procrastination. Other personalities, or features of one's personality, predispose them to put off the 'important tasks.' We will highlight these traits and discuss working methods to counter-balance this problem.

There's never a need to feel inhibited by your weaknesses, rather, learning to cooperate with them unlocks your strength and power as an individual. Give yourself the best advantages. Transform your weakness into a strength. The following are some of the personality traits and dispositions that contribute to procrastination.

Perfectionism

"Perfectionism is the setting of and striving for, very demanding standards that are self-imposed and relentlessly pursued despite this causing problems. It involves basing one's self-worth almost exclusively on how well these high standards are met"

Shafran, Egan, Wade (2010)

Consider how this would affect self-worth

Perfectionists also struggle with procrastination. Perfectionism is defined as a disposition to feel that anything less than perfect is unacceptable. To these personality types, a task must be done correctly if it is to be attempted at all. You can imagine how these minds are susceptible to falsely representing the required effort with consideration to the undertaking of a particular task. Are you noticing a pattern here? Many of the causes of procrastination described will involve how we construe the details of the task to our minds.

Let's take a deeper look. Perfectionism may seem like a positive trait or an ideal. And indeed, both applying your best initiative, and envisioning your task as being completed well, are powerful ingredients in the formula for success. However, this book constantly reminds us of the importance of balancing the traits that are already present in your behaviors and personality. Perfectionism is an imbalance that contributes to shame and lower self-esteem. Even when a perfectionist accomplishes a task, he feels dissatisfied. He believes that he could have done better, or that anyone was capable of accomplishing the task. Perfectionists degrade and diminish themselves constantly. They are their own worst enemies. While mental dialogue filled with self-criticism is highly active in these individuals, task completion and general activity may not be as a direct result of their perfectionism. This is why perfectionism is an imbalance that needs to be realigned. Unmodulated perfectionism and perfectionism tendencies will result in reduced efficiency. You will spend more energy getting less, or nothing done. In many cases, the sufferer fears inferior results and will not even make an attempt towards the effort.

If you have a perfectionist personality type, heed the following advice for better management of your tendency to procrastinate. The key principle that you must let flow into your life is acceptance. Perfectionists must learn to accept, accept, accept. If the definition of a perfectionist is to be unhappy with your achievements, then we can see that the term's definition implies its formula.

- Learn to be happy with your successes. Recognize that those with healthy self-

relationships are not critically disheartened by setbacks and other negative events.
- Learn to have flexible expectations and flexible definitions of success. Recognize that your high standards and rigid definitions of success only stifle your abilities by causing you to become idle.
- Learn to cultivate a static, unconditional form of self-confidence. Recognize that basing your self-worth on producing perfect results is a dangerous contingency

Instant gratification

Those seeking experiences that offer instant rewards, or instant gratification, represent a category of individuals that most commonly have problems with procrastination. We are faced with many tasks in the course of an average day. For instant gratification seekers, the tasks that feature rewards that can be experienced that same day will be the ones that instant gratification selects first. This preference for instant rewards is often misunderstood. These individuals come off as irresponsible and lazy. We can understand why they earn this reputation. Favoring tasks with immediate payoffs while simultaneously postponing tasks that offer future payoffs appears irresponsible from the outside looking in. These individuals seem incapable of prioritizing their goals, and at times, downright immature. Recognize, however, that this is just a particular style. Favoring tasks offering immediate rewards is, in fact, a strength depending on the world and environment in which an individual exists. For example, in environments where survival depends on the use of our fight or flight response is where persons exhibiting this personality trait thrive. Obviously, this is not the world in which most of us live in today. This misunderstood talent is, in fact, a deterring disservice in terms of planning and long-term goal setting.

If you are an instant gratification seeker, it may be helpful for you to engage your task as though it is a threat. Threats carry a high priority in the minds of instant gratification seekers. Usually, timely completion of a homework assignment, for example, will be perceived by you as a task that can be put off until later. Your mind not only views this task as one that could be completed later but also that it *should* be completed later. Your mind often makes inaccurate forecasts regarding future energy levels and motivation. Again, we address this by transforming mundane tasks, which apparently have no immediate consequence or danger, into tasks that can be seen as a fight or flight dilemma. You will find that this perception will activate your attention centers. You now construe your task to the mind as one that will threaten your survival if not addressed swiftly.

That homework assignment, for example, should be seen as a contingency for survival. Failure to complete your homework assignment will negatively impact your chances of survival, while swiftly eliminating the threat will ensure it. Truly, this is not just some imaginary way to conceptualize your task; rather, it is the reality of the situation. A realization of the urgency that underpins modern, twenty-first century tasks is what you have been lacking. It may seem like a simple problem, and fortunately for you, it is. Instant gratification seekers, you are yesterday's key to survival. You provided us with food an adequate shelter at critical and pivotal times when we're forced to contend with the natural world. In modern times, your contributions are just as necessary. Your mission now, though, is to see the modern world as an environment where survival still depends on how quickly and thoroughly you handle existential threats.

It is a completely different world, but do not become complacent. Complacency now, just as it did then, will find you fighting for your life. So, again, I say to you, when faced with a mundane task, elevate the urgency of this task by likening it to a threat in the wilderness. Use the fight option to respond to, and engage your task, and you will discover the capability to complete your task with a higher level of efficiency than those who formerly ridiculed you for lack of motivation.

Anxiety, Apathy, and Depression

Procrastination is often present in tandem with anxiety, apathy, depression, or a combination of the three. All of these affect our emotions and diminish our state of mind.

Anxiety is a feeling of worry, nervousness, or unease, typically about an imminent event or something with an uncertain outcome.

Apathy is a lack of interest, enthusiasm, or concern.

Depression is classified by chronic feelings of despondency or dejection.

The reason that any of these symptoms may be present in your life is highly varied and case dependent. We can, however, examine these definitions to gain insights into how to solve the problems we face. These symptoms are merely clues and cues, signaling the nature of the change we will need to affect in order to reintroduce harmony. These disorders and emotions can be very serious. In such cases, you should seek or continue treatment of these clinical conditions. Truly, procrastination and laziness are actually symptoms of anxiety, apathy, and depression. The treatment of these specific conditions falls outside of the scope of this book. This book is best suited for individuals experiencing mild to moderate manifestations of these conditions. Use your wisdom to assess to what degree these domains affect task completion and general behavior.

If you have mild/moderate anxiety pertaining to some project or task, see that it is part of the human experience to feel nervous when engaging a project, especially if it's a first of a kind. Do not become consumed by your uncertainty regarding specific outcomes. We can never entirely ensure future results in any case. However, we are able to influence the likelihood of certain outcomes by our actions. This will be the truth that sets you free in places you back on the road to productivity. Later, specific methods providing security to those who worry about the completion of their task will be presented. The following is the most powerful and insightful bit of knowledge about anxiety: Anxiety is excitement misunderstood. While anxiety may seem like a prohibitive trait, the realization that excitement is the true underlying emotion should help to re-encourage you. Excitement is an abundance of energy, and energy is precisely what you need to achieve your goals.

SMART Goals

Specific: A goal that is specific has distinct and separate states of success and failure which means it is already statistically more likely to be accomplished than a goal that is extremely vague.

When it comes to choosing appropriately specific goals, consider who you can turn to for help in completing the goal, the target for the goal in question, where you will need to be to attain the goal as well as when you want the goal to be completed. Finally, you will need to consider any potential restraints that will keep you from success. You will know you have the right goal in mind when you have the answer to all 6 specifics.

Measurable: A good goal is one where progress towards success can easily be measured, giving you a feeling of accomplishment and a serotonin boost every time you make another step in the right direction. With your first few goals it is extremely important to keep them measurable in order to nurture the growth of the proper neural pathways. To determine the metric of success you should be using, start by determining the easiest criteria by which you can measure success.

This metric can either be one that is based on achieving certain predetermined outcomes or one that is based on cold, hard facts, the important thing is that there are clearly defined points that can be used to ensure you are always on the right track. Early goals tend to work better when the success metric is a number that can be easily defined as it helps to be able to constantly see a stream of new progress unfolding.

Attainable: SMART goals are attainable. When it comes to setting a useful long term goal, it is important that you choose one that is both far-fetched enough to be motivational while down to earth enough that it is actually possible. If the goal that you set ends up being too easily attainable, all you will have to do is think bigger down the line which is why it will behoove you to choose something that you can expect to ultimately come relatively close to achieving at the very least.

The trick here is to pick a goal that is attainable enough to keep you working diligently at it, while not so easy that it wouldn't make sense to have sub-goals surrounding completing it successfully. While 20 years out might be a bit excessive for your current needs, everyone can benefit from a good five-year plan. If you land on a goal that is either too difficult to achieve or too easy to warrant striving towards you will find it much for difficult to work to achieve it successfully.

Realistic: A goal is realistic if it is attainable, regardless of the amount of effort required, without requiring an act of divine intervention to see them through. The ideal goal is one that is difficult enough that you will have to work for it, but not so difficult that it becomes unrealistic. Likewise, it is important to not pick easy goals as studies show that believing a goal is easily within reach is actually a detriment to your motivation to complete it.

Likewise, it is important that the goal you choose to start with is one that is going to fit into your current routine with as little overall disruption as possible. Your early goals are going to have little real self-discipline to fall back on which means you need to do everything in your power to aid them on early on for the best results. If you can make a habit from completing the task in question then you are on your way to success.

Timeframe: While a good goal contains a wide variety of important properties one of the most important is that you include a time table as to when the goal will be completed. Even the most specific, measurable, attainable and relevant goals will never be finished if you leave them open ended as you will never feel the deadline closing in and begin to work harder accordingly.

While setting the goal of going to the gym 4 times a week in order to lose 20 pounds is great assuming it is something you want to and have the free time to accomplish, if you don't set a realistic time frame, say six months from today, then you may well never get up off the couch initially because tomorrow will always seem like a viable time to start. This is not to say that once you set a timeline for a goal that timeline is set in stone; rather, the timeline is important as a motivating factor which means that as long as you are regularly working on attaining the goal there is no harm in adjusting the timeline as needed.

Chapter 4:
Cognitive Reframing

Usually, in the case of a project that is sophisticated or time-consuming, confusion and and a feeling of being overwhelmed may leave you paralyzed. There are a variety of functional aspects and high demands associated with larger projects. Individuals that are gifted at seeing the big picture are easily prone to feeling overwhelmed when considering the effort required by their large task. If your reason for procrastination comes from a lack of knowing what to do to get started, this brief section should help give you some perspective.

A practical comparison that will help reveal the nature of this problem is to see your project like it's a 1000-piece puzzle. When we sit down to work on a sophisticated puzzle like this, we do not let ourselves become overwhelmed by the effort required to piece together our puzzle. There is, on the contrary, usually no hesitation or idleness at all. Immediately, we begin applying a strategy to help us complete the puzzle. Each of us has a strategy that works best for us when solving a puzzle, but all of these strategies have something in common. First, we must take our puzzle one piece at a time. Second, we solve for all of the known elements of our puzzle. Employ the same strategy when working on your project, which features a multitude of unknowns. There will be bits and pieces of your project that you already know or have an idea about how to execute. This allows us to get the ball rolling, and to invigorate our project with a strong start. Also, the known aspects of our project begin to imply how to solve unknown aspects.

Many puzzle builders like to find the outline of the puzzle first. Likewise, try to find some outline for your project. Then, randomly select a portion of your project that seems easy or that is most appealing to you. Imagine if one of the rules of piecing together a puzzle was that you must assemble the puzzle in a left to right, and top to bottom fashion. This effort would be most frustrating and time-consuming and would result in puzzles being a much less popular pastime. Thankfully, putting together a puzzle is purely about arriving at a completed result. The same holds true in task completion. For some reason or another, we may automatically try to fulfill the details and demands of our project sequentially. The next time you are feeling confused about how to start you're a large project; remember it is but a 1000-piece puzzle. The beginning, middle, and final phases of assembling a puzzle are both stimulating and fulfilling. This is because the end result is an appreciable accomplishment achieved by observing this simple principle: Only solve for the known elements.

Rumination Period

Rumination - a deep or considered thought about something.

There is no virtue in inactivity according to Western culture. We are a busy group of people, idealizing packed schedules and being constantly productive. Keeping busy is not a bad thing in itself. Our minds and bodies are designed to be employed. We derive contentment from working and producing. Though as with all things, we will need to learn to strike a balance that best fits our condition. For those in the condition of internalized procrastination, there is an imbalance on the side of inactivity.

You guessed it; this is not a bad thing. Never worry, for it's not actually possible for you to be truly inactive. Many times, people, especially those who claim to be members of the "I work well under pressure" club, are unconsciously ruminating over their task before execution. This is actually a powerful and important process that occurs in the mind. We remember from earlier in the book that one of the tasks delegated to the unconscious mind is higher order thinking. This means as we go on about our day carrying out other tasks, our unconscious is secretly planning how to best execute the task we are procrastinating. This means rumination is one of the causes of procrastination. This is especially true in cases where, initially, we are not entirely sure of how to complete our task. Just because we didn't know exactly what to do didn't mean we gave up or lost interest in doing it, we simply sent it to another part of our minds that specializes in deep consideration, while simultaneously moving onto simpler tasks in which we already know how to carry out. This is actually a very efficient decision because it's like multitasking.

If we sat down and forced ourselves to try to complete the task and overcome our initial confusion, it is likely we would develop a poor attitude regarding the task, spend far more time trying to consciously solve dilemmas, the quality of our output would be lessened, and, to top it all off, those other smaller and more surmountable tasks we would have been able to knock out didn't get accomplished either.

Now when you realize that you are procrastinating, you may be able to diagnose the cause based on the information just shared. Also, you may now choose consciously to postpone activity for the same reason. Regardless of if you become aware of such autonomous rumination, or you consciously make the decision to ruminate over your task, it is recommended that you use these techniques to supplement this powerful process.

- Carry a notebook or notepad, a laptop or tablet computer, a smartphone with a notes app readily available.
- Periodically, use your imagination to envision yourself working on your task with ease and enthusiasm.

- Pay close attention to the details that stand out in your experiences. Your unconscious mind is constantly seeking to connect and relate its thoughts and experiences.
- Talk to others about your task.

This is not something you will need to practice. The unconscious mind already operates in this fashion. Even now as you are reading these words, your unconscious mind is working on other problems and reviewing scenarios that you have recently encountered, along with retained memories from deeper in your past. You can make this system operate to your benefit with a conscious recognition of how it works. The fact that we dream at night is proof that the mind never sleeps, is never inactive and is never lazy. Day and night, it works to make sense of the things we experience. Why should you do all the heavy lifting then? When you have a new task before you, if you are not immediately motivated to begin work on your task, shamelessly decide to spend a day or two ruminating over your task first. Postponement, in this case, may be your wisest choice.

A "Temporal Investment"

Previously, we considered the impacts of primal conditioning on some of our modern behaviors. More specifically, we discussed that in the context of survival; the mind will routinely choose the tasks that offer quick and easy returns. Under these conditions, such behavior is not regarded as laziness, but rather, a strategic approach to survival. Even being fully cognizant of the reality that survival is no longer an elemental concern, you may still find yourself favoring tasks that appeal to your desire for instant gratification. Some reserve a spiritual disposition that planning for the future is mostly frivolous, as we haven't conquered death, and tomorrow is never promised. I will not attempt to change your mind on this matter. I will suggest, however, that if your reason for procrastination is caused by an imbalance in your desire for instant gratification, that you mentally reframe what your task has to offer you.

For those that habitually postpone tasks in favor of activities that offer fun and instant rewards, it may be time to start regarding those things you procrastinate as temporal investments. The word "temporal," meaning temporary, or existing within time...

We already know that everything existing in time eventually ends. Your task will not plague you forever. You know this. You will do it for a short time, and then it will be over. The hardship incurred (if any) will dissolve away, but the benefits from having completed your task will have lasting effects that may serve you multiple times in the future.

Life for mankind has evolved so much in the last century, and this evolution has only accelerated in recent decades. Before the 20th century, the ways of life and survival changed at a much slower pace. Due to rapid modernization, it's both normal and justified to have adaptational shortcomings. Observe what these changes in your environment are and what your world requires of you. It's easy to prioritize seemingly urgent and time sensitive tasks ahead of your mundane task or long, drawn out project. Recognize this action of the mind. It is trying to make decisions to ensure your survival. The problem, however, is that we no longer face the challenges of day-to-day survival. Many living on the planet today don't have to contend with a daily fight for their lives. Instead, we now make calculated and strategic moves to ensure our futures rather than the present. In this light, we should never be put off by our tendency to favor instant gratification. It is simply the mind doing what it can to try to protect the body. Praise this behavior, but then quickly adjust your mental representation of the context and environment so your mind may serve you appropriately.

Remind yourself that all things end. You will not be tied up working on your project indefinitely. The time for it will come to an end and you will either have done the task or not. Make a temporal investment in your future.

The "It's Easy" Mentality

Some encounter an issue in which the task they wish to accomplish costs too much effort or hassle for the given payoff. Tasks failing this cost versus pay-off analysis are a very common reason for procrastination. Procrastinating the washing of a stack of dirty dishes is a classic example of this. Often, the thought of tending to the stack of dishes seems imposing, thankless, and unrewarding. A frequent procrastinator will pursue the tasks featuring high payoffs, and minimum costs. It is true that we use our imagination to envision the work that is to be performed. Envisioning or imagining yourself doing your task is a powerful part of the process of getting motivated.

So if many cases of procrastination are the result of the cost value exceeding the reward value in the equation, then we simply need to find a way to reduce one or increase the other. This chapter is going to present the methodology for reducing the cost value aspect of the equation. Many cases of procrastination are caused by negative imaginations, attitudes, and associations with the task that is to be completed. These negative associations are usually due to a person's confusion about how to get started or prepared for their task. When we don't know how to start our project, we panic and often misconstrue the details of the undertaking. We create an exaggerated image in our minds of what our project will entail. It is necessary to stabilize this imbalance if we wish to end our tendency to choose procrastination.

The image your mind creates in relation to your task is a reflection of your attitude toward the task. More specifically, it's a representation of your confidence in your abilities to complete the task. We can actually say that imagination is what determines the values in this equation, and that having constructive feelings and imaginations about your task will improve your efficiency. Likewise, imagining your task as being difficult or draining will have a negative impact on your motivation levels. Luckily, the same holds true if, and when, we imagine ourselves working diligently to complete a task. Simply picturing ourselves completing a task with ease, passion, and enthusiasm prepares and conditions us to have exactly that experience.

Envision your task as being easy. You must tell yourself that it is something that you actually can accomplish. You would not have been assigned the task by someone else if they did not believe you were capable of fulfilling it, and likewise, you would not have accepted the task if you knew ultimately you would not be able to accomplish it. This is the great news. Anything from washing those dishes, or cleaning out the pool, to being assigned some intricate project, realize that your task is not actually difficult at all. You already know what to do, how to wash the dishes, for example, you just somehow have made it seem like the task requires some exaggerated exertion of energy. You now realize that the only tough part of the task is the initiation. Doing your task is not hard or outside of your abilities. Realize the ease of your task and your feelings of reluctance will slip away.

Chapter 5:
Activity and Nutrition

If you've ever owned a dog as a pet, you have likely experienced how apparently essential taking him/her out for a daily walk can be regarding their mental health. Dogs that are confined to the house all day tend to develop strange behavioral quirks. Some breeds become downright disobedient and unruly if not given the opportunity to go out and sniff around and get exercise. Inversely, dogs that are fortunate enough to receive regular and daily walks by their owners are much better behaved and are more receptive to our commands and training. Just as dogs benefit from going on regular walks, physical activity will serve as a wonderful outlet for the human body and mind to express excess energy.

When we exercise, we improve our circulation, which delivers life-supporting oxygen to our cells. Not only this, but our minds become highly active during this time. For many people, thinking and moving occur in tandem with one another. Exercise is a great way to engage the unconscious mind. As the body reaps the rewards of our exercise, so too does our mind. If you are having trouble mustering the required focus and motivation to tackle your task, go for a run, swim, or bike ride, and evaluate the impact to your state of mind.

Regardless of whether or not you will choose to be active as a means of clearing and balancing your thoughts, it is imperative that you be mindful of your diet. Although this is mentioned second, adequate nutrition may be one of the most primary influencers to laziness, while simultaneously being the most overlooked. With the definition of laziness being the unwillingness to expend energy toward a certain task, it would be logical to conclude that perhaps the reason you are feeling energy deficient is that your body is running low on the resources that give rise to focus, concentration, and feelings of well-being.

For our ancestors, survival was not as assured as it is in modern times. Due to the lack of technology and medical treatment that is prevalent in our time, every day was a challenge to survive. The brain is wired to help ensure the survival of the entity. This wiring has been reinforced over many generations that were exposed to conditions where survival was less than guaranteed. This, perhaps, is why humans so innately seek instant gratification. Long before the technology existed to refrigerate and preserve our food, for example, the man had to hunt or gather food when he was hungry. He could not procure edible meat days, or even hours in advance as the meat would spoil make him sick. It had to be fresh. There must've been little time spent making preparations for the future for our early ancestors, as survival consumed and preoccupied all of their time. Examining our origins in this way provides some additional insight into the cause of our propensity toward instant gratification as discussed earlier, however, let's get back to nutrition.

A highly important technique employed by those faced with a survival scenario is the conservation of energy. This concept doesn't exist in modern times as, conversely, our access and consumption of food have many looking to burn excess energy as opposed to saving it. No one sits around and idles for the sake of energy conservation - at least not consciously.

In fact, just because we intake food doesn't mean that we are adequately nourished, and all too often we fill up on foods that have little or no positive impact on our energy levels and ability to focus. There are several nutritional factors that support our productivity. If you have a task that requires focus, critical thinking, or physical exertion, ensure to prime your body and mind by paying attention to these dietary aspects.

Hydration

Proper hydration entails much more than merely consuming water. Water in the body has little value if not balanced with an appropriate electrolyte level. This is because, contrary to popular belief, water itself is not conductive. Your nervous system, which includes your brain, is an electrical system. In order for the electrical current to flow through water, minerals (mainly salt) must be present.

It is common to see people flocking to stimulants like coffee and energy drinks to supplement Energy and concentration levels. These substances are popularly sought because they do indeed work - but only for a time. If you've ever been a victim of coffee addiction, then you are familiar with the effects of its hit-or-miss feature ingredient: caffeine. In the beginning, and on seemingly random days, they may have a high efficacy with regards to maintaining your focus and motivation. However, we know that caffeine is a diuretic, and diuretics draw water out of the body. Making matters worse, you may have believed that an appropriate countermeasure to this effect was to simply replenish the water that was being lost by drinking more. This tactic, on the contrary, only exacerbated the problem by then stripping precious minerals from the body. The end result of such a combination left you devoid of the two components that support optimum hydration. If you have ever reached the point in your day where an additional cup of coffee only left you feeling jittery and unfocused, it was likely that you destroyed your hydration level and are now working with the nervous system in which the signals have become weak and incoherent.

Caffeine supplements are great tools to use in moderation, however, recognize they're temporary sources of energy that have a degenerative effect on our bodies hydration, which eventually affects our ability to think and focus. It is ideal to not depend on caffeine to motivate you into action, however, if the consumption of caffeine is nonnegotiable for you, it is recommended to add juicy fruits to your diet as they will re-incorporate water, minerals, vitamins, unrefined sugars, and in some cases antioxidants. Also, since the water that comes from fruits is contained within, fruits offer a time-release advantage over strictly drinking a glass of water.

"Natural Health News — If you just can't think straight, a glass of water may help get your brain working again.

The human brain is made up of around 85% water. When you are not properly hydrated the effects can be felt in your brain as symptoms like headaches, poor concentration, and reduced short-term memory. Even your ability to perform arithmetic and the rapidity of your psychomotor skills can be reduced. This is due to the fact that dehydration causes the level of energy production in the brain to decrease...

Staying hydrated, thus, may be a way of "freeing up of attentional resources", say the researchers in the journal Frontiers in Human Neuroscience.

Earlier studies in adults have suggested that dehydration can affect mental performance and mood. For instance, in one study in 2012 found that being even slightly dehydrated is enough to cause moodiness, problems concentrating, headaches and fatigue in women and studies in children have suggested water consumption can improve memory.

Researchers still can't explain why drinking water appears to have beneficial effects on some cases, but negative effects in others."

-Staff Writer, 18 November 2013, Natural Health News, "Drinking Water Improves Focus, Reaction Time"

B vitamins

Luckily, there are many foods that feature B vitamins. Depending on the nature of your diet, you may have no problem getting a sufficient amount of B vitamins in your diet. If not, a quick search on the web will offer many choices. Of which, you will surely be able to find multiple sources that are both palatable and affordable. B vitamins primarily help the body convert the foods we consume into usable energy for the body.

"B vitamins are often called the energy vitamins, but they are more like keys that unlock it.

Fatigue, irritability, poor concentration, anxiety and depression—all can be signs of a B vitamin deficiency. That's because compounds in the B complex are needed for everything from the healthy maintenance of brain cells to the metabolism of carbohydrates, the brain's source of fuel. Bs are also necessary for the production of neurotransmitters, which regulate mood and conduct messages through the brain.

The B complex includes B1 (thiamine), B2 (riboflavin), B3 (niacin), B6, pantothenic acid, biotin, B12 and folate, also known as folic acid on vitamin bottles. It also includes choline, a nutrient found in eggs that are needed to produce cell membranes and may slow age-related memory loss.

Which B is most important? It's impossible to say.

"They all have important roles," says Roxanne Moore, a registered dietitian at the Maryland Department of Education and a spokeswoman for the American Dietetic Association. A varied, healthy diet of lean meats, colorful vegetables and whole grains will usually cover the bases.

The subgroup of B6, B12 and folate is the subject of much research. Sufficient intake lowers rates of birth defects, cardiovascular disease, depression, dementia and Alzheimer's disease. The three work together and even marginal deficiencies have large effects.

B6 and B12 contribute to the myelin sheath around nerve cells, which speeds signals through the brain. B12 and folic acid together are needed for making normal cells, including blood cells. Inadequate B12 or folic acid can yield blood cells unable to carry vital oxygen to the brain.

These three Bs aid in the manufacture of the excitatory neurotransmitter GABA, as well as serotonin and dopamine, neurotransmitters that regulate mood. All three neurotransmitters regulate each other, but the ways they work in concert or against each other are only beginning to be understood.

Only rarely are the effects of a B vitamin deficiency clear-cut. The Centers for Disease Control reported that two children had severe motor and language skill delays because of a deficiency in vitamin B12. They had both been breastfed by vegan mothers who were also deficient in B12.

The vitamin occurs naturally only in animal products, although many cereals and soy products are fortified with B12, among others. Both children quickly improved after eating a new diet, but both also had lingering language and motor problems a year after treatment."

-Willow Lawson, April 2, 2003, "Vitamin B: A Key to Energy"

Antioxidants

Antioxidants detoxify the body through some process of removing or breaking down free radicals.

"Because they have one or more unpaired electrons, free radicals are highly unstable. They

scavenge your body to grab or donate electrons, thereby damaging cells, proteins, and DNA (genetic material). The same oxidative process also causes oils to become rancid, peeled apples to turn brown, and iron to rust.

It is impossible for us to avoid damage by free radicals. Free radicals arise from sources both inside (endogenous) and outside (exogenous) our bodies. Oxidants that develop from processes within our bodies form as a result of normal aerobic respiration, metabolism, and inflamemation. Exogenous free radicals form from environmental factors such as pollution, sunlight, strenuous exercise, X-rays, smoking and alcohol. Our antioxidant systems are not perfect, so as we age, cell parts damaged by oxidation accumulate...

Antioxidants block the process of oxidation by neutralizing free radicals. In doing so, the antioxidants themselves become oxidized. That is why there is a constant need to replenish our antioxidant resources.

How they work can be classified in one of two ways:

Chain-breaking - When a free radical releases or steals an electron, a second radical is formed. This molecule then turns around and does the same thing to a third molecule, continuing to generate more unstable products. The process continues until termination occurs -- either the radical is stabilized by a chain-breaking antioxidant such as beta-carotene and vitamins C and E, or it simply decays into a harmless product.

Preventive - Antioxidant enzymes like superoxide dismutase, catalase and glutathione peroxidase prevent oxidation by reducing the rate of chain initiation. That is, by scavenging initiating radicals, such antioxidants can thwart an oxidation chain from ever setting in motion.

They can also prevent oxidation by stabilizing transition metal radicals such as copper and iron.

The effectiveness of any given antioxidant in the body depends on which free radical is involved, how and where it is generated, and where the target of damage is. Thus, while in one particular system an antioxidant may protect against free radicals, in other systems it could have no effect at all. Or, in certain circumstances, an antioxidant may even act as a "pro-oxidant" that generates toxic oxygen species."

-Robin Brett Parnes, "Antioxidants: What You Need to Know"

Free radicals are just poisons or toxins, and these slow and inhibit the body's performance. They interfere with energy levels and cause the body to operate at a reduced efficiency. Antioxidants can be considered a brain food since the brain is one of the regions of the body impacted by high toxicity levels. If you drink, just think of how well your brain cooperates with you when intoxicated by alcohol. Though at a lesser degree, the same principle is in operation inside a body with a high toxicity level. Supplement your diet with antioxidants to gain a boost in mental clarity and wellbeing.

Fats

Fats have acquired a bad reputation due to corporate interests. This is another topic entirely, but it is important here for you understand that fats are responsible for the development of the brain in Homo sapiens. Fats are globally important to the body, and you may remember from biology the prevalence of "lipids" when talking about cells. Fats are almost like proteins to the brain if the brain were a muscle. The demonization of fatty foods by various forms of propaganda has successfully contributed to a reduction in fat consumption in western civilizations. This, indeed, is likely one of the primary causes, second only to hydration, that laziness is such a relevant and pertinent modern-day problem. Quality, "healthy fats" such as Omega fatty acids should be preferred. However, fats from any source are recommended versus consuming none at all.

"1. Polyunsaturated Fat
Polyunsaturated fats contain the essential fatty acids (EFAs) omega-3 and omega-6. Our brains need these fats to function properly (studies also show that eating high quantities of omega-3 fatty acids are linked to reduced rates of major depression, but our bodies are unable to produce them. This means it's important that we include these fat sources in our diets.

2. DHA
An omega-3 fatty acid, DHA has been shown to help brain functions like memory, speaking ability, and motor skills. Increasing dietary levels of omega-3s have been shown to help

improve conditions such as depression, bipolar disorder, and ADHD.

3. Saturated Fat
Saturated fat is actually one of the main components of brain cells and is therefore necessary for healthy brain function. In one study, it was found that people who ate more saturated fat reduced their risk for developing dementia by 36 percent. Saturated fat also provides benefits for the liver and immune system and helps maintain proper hormone balance."

-David Landau, "How Eating Fat Can Make You Smarter"

Unrefined sugars

Although least important, glucose levels are a contributor to our perceived energy levels and ability to focus. They also stimulate our brain's reward system, which is uplifting. This one is easy to overdo since we really don't need much of it to produce the desired results. Also, it is imperative that this intake of sugar comes from an unrefined, natural origin. Candies, confections, juices, and sodas should all wait until you have completed your task. They're great for celebrating your success in the end, but they will inhibit your performance prior to task completion.

By now, you are beginning to understand that by not meeting the dietary requirements that enable optimum performance of your body and mind, your unconscious may revert to primal conditioning and survival tactics. Lacking the necessary biological resources, the body may assume that it is in a survival situation, and thereby autonomously select idleness to preserve physical resources in an effort to ensure your survival. If you are not doing your part tending to the nourishment of your body, survival mode may be the cause of your laziness, and consequently, your procrastination of the given task.

Conclusion

Thank you for making it through to the end of *Laziness: How to Turn your Life Around with Proven Methods to Overcome Procrastination, Laziness, and Lack of Motivation*, let's hope it was informative and able to provide you with all of the tools you need to achieve your goals, whatever it is that they may be. Just because you've finished this book doesn't mean there is nothing left to learn on the topic, expanding your horizons is the only way to find the mastery you seek.

In this book, you have learned to distinguish between laziness and procrastination. They are not the same thing. Laziness usually causes us to procrastinate, but we don't always procrastinate out of laziness. There are many reasons we procrastinate. With the information presented here, you have the tools you need to cooperate with your tendencies rather than fight them. We now understand cooperation is our only option because fighting will cause our lazy and procrastination tendencies to persist.

Even when we do procrastinate, it is not all bad. Our unconscious minds will still engage with the material while we tend to other things. Although this is a passive process, we can influence it. Use this power to your advantage.

The advice for overcoming procrastination is plentiful. A variety of techniques and battle tactics exist to assist you in your management of the subject. Some of these may actually serve you for a time, while others may not. The insights offered by this book attempt to nudge you closer toward the direction of understanding yourself, your needs, and your behaviors. This is where lasting change takes place. Once you realize that laziness is a manifestation of some imbalance residing within, you will then hold the keys to self-treatment. Use the knowledge you have gained from this book to get some initial orientation with the matter. Though realize, this book is a practical guide that shares information on how to take the reins and author treatment methods that best suit your needs and conditions.

Let's reinforce one final time why the use of formalized techniques to combat procrastination is ultimately futile. There is a technique known as covert hypnosis. It can be applied to influence the self and others through the manipulation of the unconscious mind. Most commonly, though, it's used to influence an external party. With proper application of the concepts of covert hypnosis, the influencer can effectively change the views and perceptions of his victim. This gives the influencer the power to persuade the target to accept offers and propositions that they would not have selected if this coercion weren't present. The implications run deep. The mind can be hacked and exploited to observe its environment in different ways. Investigate "speed seduction," "conversational hypnosis," or "auto suggestion" for more information about how this topic works. The only problem with using these "mind hacks" is the results can last only as long as the victim is exposed to the suggestions of the hypnotist. The same holds true for techniques used to fight against procrastination. For lasting changes, take on the strategies bestowed in these chapters.

Finally, if you enjoyed this book, please consider leaving a review on the platform. Reviews are one of the simplest ways to support the work of self-published authors.

Thank you, and good luck!

Printed in Poland
by Amazon Fulfillment
Poland Sp. z o.o., Wrocław